The Blues Drink
Your Dreams Away

Selected Poems
(1983-2018)
by John Macker

Stubborn Mule Press
Devil's Elbow, MO
stubbornmulepress@gmail.com

Copyright (c) John Macker, 2018
First Edition 1 3 5 7 9 10 8 6 4 2
ISBN: 978-1-946642-74-5
LCCN: 2018911573

Design, edits and layout: Jeanette Powers
Cover image: Jon Lee Grafton
Author photo: Annie Macker
All rights reserved. No part of this publication may be reproduced or transmitted in any form or by any means, electronic or mechanical, including photocopying, recording or by info retrieval system, without prior written permission from the author.

Some of these poems appeared in the following books:

For the Few (broadside. Denver: Passion Press, Bowery 36, 1983), *The First Gangster* (Glenwood Springs: Long Road Press, 1994), *Burroughs at Santo Domingo* (Bernal, NM: Long Road/La Cantera Press, 1998.) *Adventures in the Gun Trade* (Bernal, NM: Long Road/La Cantera Press, 2004) *Woman of the Disturbed Earth.* (Lafayette, CO: Turkey Buzzard Press, 2007) *Las Montañas de Santa Fe* (Denver: DCArt Press, 2009) and *Underground Sky* (Lafayette, CO: Turkey Buzzard Press, 2009), *Disassembled Badlands* (Turkey Buzzard Press, 2014), *Blood in the Mix* (with Lawrence Welsh, Lummox Press, 2015)

Special thanks to Molly Wagoner, Jeanette Powers and Jason Ryberg.

CONTENTS

The Sagebrush of the Glaciers / 1

Now is the hour of the assassins / 2

Scorpion is the Patron Saint of Gunslingers / 3

Call Me the Doc Holliday of Language / 5

Dispossessed / 7

The Magic Circle / 9

Cochise: A Meditation / 11

Endgame / the Beginning / 14

Loba Sonnet / 18

August, Augusto, Augustus / 19

another morning on earth / 20

for the few / 22

ventriloquist poem / 24

Burning Mountain Windy Morning's Rap / 25

Peckinpah's Typewriter / 26

Blues for Pajarito Plateau / 28

when we were once rivers, no more / 30

Descanso* / 32

A Day in the Life of an Altar Boy / 33

first light / 35

poem to help you quit smoking / 36

The fate of Lorca's bones / 37

no exit sutra / 39

beyond geography / 40

what the scalphunter said / 41

A Couple of James McMurtry Songs Later / 42

the roaring stillness across open ground / 44

Cochise's Confession / 46

nirvana desperados / 47

the blues drink yr dreams away / 49

Somewhere Between Arikara and Ft. Union / 51

Borrowed time in Chaco Canyon / 52

jaguar sighting in northern Mexico / 54

Territorial Sunday Best / 56

global warning / 58

Winter Solstice / 60

Sierra Oscura / 62

The Day I Die / 65

La Risa Café / 69

Japanese Volcano / 70

tracking the words / 71

after The Fall of America / 73

Sacred Clown / 74

August in the Spanish Earth / 76

Paris Elegy #1 / 77

Paris Elegy #2 / 78

Paris Elegy #3 / 79

Mexico Elegy / 80

Midwinter's day / 81

Angels Broken Down in Denver / 83

Artaud in Mexico / 87

The Terminal Bar and Café / 89

vespers / 90

Creeley / 91

Ventriloquist Rock (Colorado) / 92

This book is dedicated to Fred Haberlein
and Frank T. Rios.

...how did you come to me to lay mothwings of song to burn on my tongue?

-Luis Alberto Urrea

The Sagebrush of the Glaciers

Absinthe was Verlaine's unraveling, no doubt. I smelled it on his clothing in Brussels, that winter, when the ice formed like lines of coke on the river's shore. In the mutual hell of their hotel room, where they could see their breaths, he introduces a gun into what's left of his relationship with young Rimbaud. A gun! He shoots the poet in his hand. Meanwhile, the ancient radiator hisses and clangs like the edge of civilization at the end of time, all night long. Especially when it snows across the city and the nighttime temperature drops treacherously below freezing.

It is still snowing, January, seven a.m. I can barely see the clock tower but I can hear it chime, a chime as frozen as a communion wafer, tolling each naked hour, a heart rhythm traveling effortlessly through the thin winter air.

His young lover, immortal Bard, calls the cops and Verlaine goes to jail. He writes letters, masturbates, repents and in 1875, visits with Rimbaud one final time. Rimbaud tells him that cruel absinthe is the sagebrush of the glaciers.

This time, no blood is exchanged between them.

Yes, in the end, absinthe is the older poet's unraveling.

Now is the hour of the assassins.
                    -Rimbaud

For Thomas McGuane

Crossing the border
the gunman is just a tiny
hangover on the horizon,
chilled to the marrow,
inclement weather to the north,
disembodied morning of Prometheus,
men with guns moving through
time and space, disappearing
into the earth, settling in casitas,
behind stones.
His grandfather a coal miner so
his father could be a teacher
so he could be a killer.
Wipes a snotty nose on his bare knuckle.
Remembers agave is my birth flower,
and there is a reassuring night pollen
shed by stars on all ponies
so they should never fear thunder or
spend an eternity
underground,
dreaming.

Scorpion is the Patron Saint of Gunslingers

To see William exit out of the feral dusk
dusty as a cave scroll
is to sense planetary discords unfurl,
just how the prairie commoner measures
self against this sinewy wraith
time freezes and then bakes unceremoniously
in the heat.

Existential backwater of a vignette occurs among
the rude dust devils down and dirty
beneath the stars: abominable Eucharist of a
moon rises over Shiprock.
The memory of a boyhood grosbeak
bathing in a trash can lid: he keeps tied in a
tobacco pouch so the wind won't
blow it all away.

Billy, melodious in the dark, riding to his special doom
stops to offload Bob Olinger's shotgun,
a love letter from Serafina,
a beat copy of the Iliad,
one forlorn shirt stolen from a Chinese laundry,
the last of the water until Chaco Canyon.
Betrayed by enemies and friends,
offloads a solitary prayer:

O Longest of the Longriders,
why have you made me ride this
disembodied dream into hell? I am
soledad. No answers.
No anguish.
No wind.
Only stillness and the sky scorpion inanimate
against the desert blackness, extremities
linked across light years,

patron saint of this motherless child.

Call Me the Doc Holliday of Language
-for Tony Scibella

Of misanthropic scorpions, dust dervishes
dry rivers,
the psilocybin horizon,
diseases of the lung
have no voice in this outback
of an era:
I witnessed the fall of the South,
in Colorado, I heard my disembodied
voice in the tall pine
thunderheaded she-rain.
I move from one incandescent
quick draw to another seduced
with the knowledge that *this*
is more an occult gesture
than gun hand.

I speak Latin.
I've opened Leonardo's notebook
to where it says The Last Supper.
In the dark of the bar,
three fingers of sour mash,
I bend over the glowing pages
like a high priest.

I am the voice of the wasteland,
the wasted, the outgunned, the
disenfranchised,
the black hollyhock,
the mockingbird's psychedelic
soundtrack to the simple act
of me, riding my pony
across the movies as a kid.

Dispossessed

We went down to Mexico to
stare our way into the heart
of the heart of the Seri sunset,
imagine wise harvest fish
totems to the desert gods built
of saltwater, shells
and the feminine. Their
footprints incarnate
in the sand.

I stood still as an organ pipe
Seri dusk, Sea of Cortez and
it's primal and ecstatic while back
home a poet's sunset is
fertile with ritual.

Fill our dispirited lungs with
sea air,
say a prayer:
Neptune rules drugs and war
here as well as there.

And when it all gets to be too much
when I want to behave in civilization
like Gregory Corso behaved at Duchamp's

house, puking all over it and
cutting off his necktie with a knife,
I want to be the last American
standing on the beach,
dispossessed, emptied of rancor
like a ransacked purse.
Temporarily angelic in the cosmos
where a mountain of vaporized
building is not another metaphor
for decay.

The Magic Circle

Inventing the unknown calls for new forms.
                                        -Rimbaud

Billy awakens hung over on a field of smoking
flowers, ascertains immediately, this don't
mean shit,
a cry in the dark more crow
than human comes from the back
of his own throat.
Sees his early death at the hand of
a once-upon-a-friend, not a vagabond death
among strangers in a strange city
that aches in its own wilting steel.
Billy will consult his small shaking
hands for spiritual direction.

Humanity in the saloon mirror is a
white wedding in a foreign desert death-
bombed from above with a cry more human
than crow. As they fall like chess pieces,
they say once they run out of bombs they'll drop
our dead children on us and out of the debris
a micaceous poet comes to life.

William stares into the mirror crystal ball
7 a.m., at the two chunks of topaz
where his eyes used to be,
while Abyssinian Arthur's eyes now resemble
a twin brother's, commiserate:

My heart has been stabbed by grace.
Upon reflection, salutes his reflection,
checks his gun hand reflexes, pours
another shot of absinthe into a yellow gourd.
He's ridden the magic circle: Lincoln, Ft. Sumner,
Anton Chico, Las Vegas, Santa Fe,
Marseilles, Paris, Mexico, and back to this
dry place in the mirror,
fondles the bullet once plucked from Rimbaud's
holy wrist, yes, the same fired by Verlaine
now fixed and private forever around his
red neck, with a thin length of
Spanish leather.

He knows only his small hands
move through the world with the
alacrity of sunflowers, in spite of this
truncated teen angst death wish of a
life staring sober back at him in the mirror.
The dark sky is every face he killed with
sulfurous hot breath that blows
another season of hell
across the desert.

Cochise: A Meditation

The only thing we had in common was
                    SURROUNDED BY AMERICA

Feeling the mystical smoke of border wildfires
filling the sky to the south,
he wipes his eyes, making a point
to his morning warriors, greased up for
the day's belligerence, arms spread
like
    THIS
standing arms akimbo on a pyramid
of boulders.

When under the gun
become a shadow of yourself   survive.

He communicates with the sheer volume
of his presence. He speaks in metaphor
for an entire civilization wired to the desert.
Because he was betrayed by the disturbed red ant
hill of American language,
he never surrendered, signed no white-
eye forked-tongue document,
wouldn't pose for a photograph,
had the magic animal
beating in his chest.

Was a transpersonalist because bacchic
celebrations drinking bluecoat moonshine at
Fort Bowie were dirty dancing and dangerous fun.
Cochise became the most cunning and feared
mobile arbiter of molecular gringo doom this
side of the solar Rio Grande.

Didn't require mescaline visions of his own secret
death because it wafted up from the black fissures
of home on its own, bereft of all superstition and mystery,
whenever the soldiers arrived already stunned silly
by an afternoon of pitiless sun.

WELCOME TO THE DRAGOONS!
Women, children and dogs running like space ghosts
to your left,
Los Hombres Invisible firing your own guns at you with
the sun at their backs on your right,
this is a good day to die bluecoat, belly shot
about a dozen times because it's an even number.
Attracting a mob of flies, torso leaking American blood,
entrails and treaties, we've removed
your tongue, trooper, so you
won't say bad things about us in the afterlife.

His surroundings surrounded: sometimes
in cottonwood dream he'd
remember the mountains that invented him

and protected him
in the blue rare falling rain,
and the voice in the dream of his future whispered
from the blackness between stars.

His surroundings hissed like summer snakes and
in this Chiricahua heat, even New York sidewalks wilt
as if being scolded by the universe.
Cochise, his surroundings surrendered,
rebel incarnate,
danger bird,
kisses his wife and sons for the last time:
tell them I died an old man.

Endgame / the Beginning

1.

This is a coda.
In language that speaks the
last of a wild life in the
wilderness, from the cradle in
Dakota to ignoble violent
death to burial high on the plains,
(at my funeral my enemies ate
wild mushrooms.)
A wild life spent expending these
few natural
resources, our primitive but
spiritual energies surviving and
transcending the code of the west
writ in blood sacrifice that always
flows downhill, flossing the land-
scape crimson regardless of politics or
the color of your synagogue,
Capilla or *morada*—

The language of death, the silence
of the night air throbbing with a billion
luminous astral bodies,
a lone rider loveless in the winter
chill is still music in any village

on any world, if you're human and if you
bleed, this is the last white page your
life is writ on.

2.

The prairie will divulge all our bones in
the end like the discovery of a new solar system,
poking through the fabric of the Mescalero sky.
One night, a black hole molested and then
devoured an innocent star not far from my woodpile.

3.

I'll always remember the towering cottonwoods
of my feral youth,
a canopy of shimmergold
leaves in the cool spring breeze,
their dream roots probing ancient ground,
deep in the womb of the Gila.
At Bosque Redondo, before my time, the
trees shadowed the Navajo with limbs of a
grave legacy. They said to them:
your whispers will come,
have grace.
A dream of old barking Indian dogs vaults
a coyote fence at sunset,
follows them en masse back to Chinle.

If not,
they throw themselves,
grieving like the April wind into the
hidden muddy
waters of the Pecos.

4.

My devotion to her is incendiary and
bright as a star. In her chest,
an angel's heart broke in the
generic damnation of my short, whoring life.
I read to her Sonnet IV:
Then, let not winter's ragged hand deface
In thee thy summer . . .
We went on.
Always will.
Hurling occult shadows of
ourselves at the bloody future,
riding brave-hearted into the morass
of pre-emptive war!

5.

Everywhere, desert. Mindless,
wind raked, mysterious, witness to savagery,
wicked bright, blushing, fearless, dry as bone,
scalphunted, angel of wastelands:

the northern Sonora villages were
as scarfaced and besieged
as any Khe San,
that birthed homeless Catholic
fantasy pistoleros out of
the baked pavement.
Drawn down to you, the cosmos connects
us with the edge of the world.
The night I was born a raven saw
its shadow and
the moon recognized herself in
a barrel of rain.

They call me the god of whisky priests,
presidents and exotic gunmen,
here lies the coda.
You can call me William.

Loba Sonnet

I once drank brandy with a woman
Who lived in a tipi inside a hybrid wolf
Enclosure near the foothills of the
Guadalupe mountains. After a few sips she said
In a husky voice: *I want you to do to me what
China did to Tibet.* I replied,
Well, that can't have a happy ending.
I'm not into endings, she said. After a few more
Sips, she said, *I want you to do to me what the
Republicans are going to do to the EPA.* I
Smiled at her: *I think there's beginning to be too many
People involved here.* She touched my cheek. *You
Seem like a nice man but hurry up,
I have to get back to my wolves.*

August, Augusto, Augustus

I was down at the San Juan exit
listening to Bob Dylan on the car radio
singing
high water everywhere
Black Mesa
Trinity Site,
Afghanistan,
high solstice voodoo chant
for rain on this
moon-bewitched desert,
    parched, down deep into my roots:
my history,
a shadow passenger,
a heap of dream bones and
the only moisture on the Jornada del
Muerto was my wife's
hummingbird tattoo of a kiss.

High above,
a pair of turkey vultures
float, trailed by a blue thunderhead
of endless war,
one with a patch of wing
feathers missing,
wheeling in lazy cursives above the
wavering scent of rain.

another morning on earth

finishing the last of this lonely coffee,
rain & the existential a.m.
               world of the map
rolled out
across my knees,
                 finger pointing:
I've been there!
& there: someday we'll be
& there where Roosevelt met
the sphinx
there's the Crimea & marked
in red all the wars
that went south.
I follow the vein of Route 66
where they spread
some bohemian's lonely ashes.

Here, north of me
Wyoming is held hostage by
an indifferent heaven
to the south:
the mighty saguaro suffers a
human struggle.
(My finger finds the latest tsunami!)

Here, where there is dawn all around me,
somebody someplace begins
another night on earth:
Africa, Paris, Greece & maybe
there's a woman,
map of the world on her knees,
her finger drops off the coast &
finds the ancient narwhal
from there she follows the blue
highway to my home town,
her imagination finds my street,
      I've telegraphed the

latitude & longitude of
my belief in mornings
& in her mind's eye she smells the
coffee & knows we're not alone.

for the few

a quiet appraisal of my times
in a dreary wonder of
neon men
the song
is the real work.

Formed of wood, whisky,
brain & glass shards,
rusty nails,
last night's blue aviary,
clay,
some things aberrant.

The work of life
after work
by carved fingers &
the dreams that come down
after hours
sure
can be felt.

How it is
what I do
once said
& I choked it down
needing more

of what I am
that what I could be
or wanted.

The message, buds
left at the bar
in the glass
on top the tip
message for the few
& out the back door
short walk to the truck
days biz done.

ventriloquist poem

I've come here
up the boreen
to work the word,
form the sound,
on the mountain,
conifer god,
bewitched by years
& eyes
to learn again from the bone,
the watersmeet,
where I'm revived
with the gift
& something that I bring
to learn all over:
elusive wapiti
buffalo creek,
conifer wind,
a god who throws his voice.

Burning Mountain Windy Morning's Rap

I told myself
to stop, smell the sky
for once or
imagine what this garden
used to be
now
all cobwebby & covered with
muddy frost.
The old fence leans into the earth
like neglected teeth,
a westerly brings in the birds & morning
rain, my dog
digs a hole in the primordial ooze &
buries all of our ancestors there.

The morning wind blows through me like
a wet kiss & I'm out the front gate,
memory no longer the sweet death
it used to be,
as old Jack and I move on
to other digs,
where a warm woman winters in the heart
& for every bird
for every garden
every wind

there's the summer of on old dog's smile
I'll remember it in.

Peckinpah's Typewriter

I've ascribed all sorts of
snakebit tequila
mysticism to it:
unearthed from a summer arroyo
placed on a flat stone
in a clearing,
battered keys,
deformed reddish with rust,
as if dropped
from Purgatory but
still sizzling with stories of
outcast border burnouts, last
gasp novels written
on the homicidal edge of
Barstow in
motel rooms that smell
of weaponized rhetoric and the
apocalypse.
The journey of the frayed soul of
Alfredo Garcia into the doomed heart
of the Sierra Madre where
exiled American nightmares
roam.

Upon which the betrayal and
gangland slaying of Jesus was
reported on a breathless day of
drifting wind not unlike today–
a group of us standing around it
as if it was the last literary
relic of the industrial age
unearthed in the weeping desert
moonshine of New Mexico.

Who couldn't imagine Bloody Sam
with Billy the Kid night sweats or
maybe Willa Cather pecking out
the heartbeat of the archbishop
on its rust-caked idiot savant keys?
Or Michael Herr's dispatches from hell;
or nativity of *The Hustler.*

Blues for Pajarito Plateau

I took a walk in the winter drizzle,
Los Alamos obscured by clouds,
the place to the west where Borges pulled
his dream revolver and exultantly
killed the gods–
I can feel the presence of the secrets
factory, its sullen modernity,
starless shadow history,
beneath its face habitual bomb dreamers
aflame underground, their deep toxic
bones moistened by the heat and the last
breath of El Niño.

In my early twenties
when a protest was still a protest,
I listened with granola-hearted mothers
to Corso read *Bomb*
on mountain lawns
of eternal light. When
sitting on the railroad tracks
of Rocky Flats was a privilege and
necessity, shoulder to shoulder
hair to hair with bohemian youth
stars praying
for spiritual guidance in the silvery
handcuffed rains
of a Colorado summer.

Pajarito,
        Pajarito,

starstruck mesa in the clouds;
someday you'll be de-veined
of your ticking arroyos
and the ancient dissected Bandelier
ash will forever be the earth
within us, beyond us.

when we were once rivers, no more

summer douses the birds
with lethargy, the wind hardly feels
like the wind at all
                         but something that
wrestles the heat to the ground
to lizard eye level and down below,
the guileless dry embudo has more staying
power than the dead.
Past misanthropes like Kit Carson or
Jack Spicer have left my old adobe house
a legendary drunken wreck, scattered their
ashes across this northern desert
& dusted their words:
                         time does not
finish a poem.

But waits for rain like it waits for death,
lizard scours the cacti for moisture
then scampers under my stock tank
for shade.
In Tehran, a girl, full of love,
falls to the street, shot in the heart.
I watch a tarantula hawk drag a paralyzed
orb weaver 50 yards to
her burrow. Her memory of rivers is
as misshapen as mine, it's as if this

big heat has wrestled time to the ground
while death
dusts itself off,
kneels at desert's edge,
cupped hands
cool rain to the mouth.

*Descanso**

A few miles south of
Vegas,
        skull whispers of dust
        blow
     across the asphalt,

all that's left
legible in this
drought:

the sunlight
          swarms over this
roadside *descanso,*

a simple cross
frayed white paint
short distance from the
shoulder of the road

sun-sharpened cross shadow etches
a tell-tale crossroads,
Coronado's horse path or
on some summer's day
the departed transmogrify
into spirited memory or
              myth

emboldened by cruel fate.

*Spanish for a cross or wreath etc marking the roadside spot where a person was last alive.

A Day in the Life of an Altar Boy

Christmas at Saint Patrick's Cathedral
for delinquent angels singing Away In The
Manger a cappella with the choir,
the crèche was alive, torpid
with solemnity,
the church smelled like pine boughs.

I didn't realize my exile
standing with tremble bone colt knees
on the December deep freeze streets of Denver
Sister Margaret Mary
betrothed to Jesus
in numinous black
laughed & waved at anything that
moved that Christmas Eve. Across Colfax,
a group of older kids held up hand made signs
that bobbed like frosted windows
looking out onto Armageddon,
excoriating America
for the bombing of Vietnam.

    I'm out in the churning wind of New Mexico,
a cup of breakfast tea trembling in
my hand, the latest war of the new
century casts its underworld glow across
the frozen tarn.

I want to tell God's mirror
I haven't been a Catholic for years
but I believe in
Apache arrowheads,
hiking across soaring mountain
streams, Joe Strummer & The Clash,
the changing seasons of work & peace,
solstice dusks with two good dogs,
a life lived softly on the edge
bereft of rancor,
Elegiac Feelings American
a desert river.

first light

I let Diego out at first light,
felt so finite under fading stars,
I heard a distant dog's bark carried
on the breeze
from the village, it
sounded like Bill's bark, a
soul mate I just buried and at that
moment

dawn was a maroon thing of beauty,
the crown of the sun
appeared
hurling sparks,
loss became a river that
flowed away from me
and near the river
a coyote yipped a frenzy
of dawn songs

the wolves of Afghanistan must've heard
and replied:
here are the ruins of war.

Loss is mostly everywhere
but dawn
spills its fiery light misted up
forever young
across all the rivers of earth.

poem to help you quit smoking

Breathe deep the
raw December night air,
hike through porous clouds to
a distant summit until you
cough like Doc Holliday.

Stop reading The Nation and
memorize the Fourteen Precepts Of
Engaged Buddhism.
Crossword puzzles.
Host a Yul Brynner film festival.
Think green,
join the revolution and
become addicted to change.
Chew gum from exotic gum trees.
Take heroin
because
a cold turkey in hand is
worth
two in the bush.

The fate of Lorca's bones

The headline read
Poet Lorca's Bones To Be Exhumed
After 72 Years
The next day we were out in Chaco Canyon with
the sand-colored lizards,
the chamisa loosed upon
the earth, the howling,
Janus-faced coyotes
who rarely
see their breaths-
some days we age like vandalized
petroglyphs, other days
we are forgiven for most everything,
in polite degrees,
drawn down into the method
of ourselves;
to emerge at first light from the
cold tent
just as a pair of canyon wrens
skitter up the cliff wall
    dawn feeding
high up
where the badlands
cool the mind.

Hiked the mesas for miles, Tsin
Kletsin, Hungo Pavi,
Kin Kletso,

The desiccated walls of secret ruins
amok with bone whispers,
Lorca, as the sun consumes all this silence,
I can hear the guns blazing.

   Stopped at a stone circle,
formed prayers out of dust
and sunlight
tiny yellow snakeweed star clusters below
zero, pointillist black canvas
Lorca and Mercury in retrograde-
in a dream I was a kid and brought home a jar
of night sky
to my long lost mother,
this is how I feel about America.
A flycatcher trills up the blue morning. I
look around at the tough survivors
greasewood,
      desert saltbush

to an exhumed Lorca
beatitude is forgiveness.

no exit sutra

The autumn leaf is emblazoned by spring's belief.
-Kenneth Patchen

first flakes of snow on Pecos Baldy,
but down here, October perspires
like a gravedigger unearthing the
last remains of summer;
prairie rattler's
last hurrah in the shade,
there,
coiled dreaming of earth free
of human antipathy,
primordial, unvarnished buzzing
trickster music of no exit,
will never be among the
disappeared, as the dogs and
I back slowly towards the road.

The whistling breeze shakes the
gold leaves loose,
the pinyon jays
shriek like renegade
witches
of jazz.

beyond geography

I thought of the Sangres
like a lover,
low green graceful range
a nativity
beyond geography

we are this open work
between words
just a pair of stone desert
eccentrics
sipping cervezas,
chatting up Borges, the
blind Argentinian
underneath the imaginary virga

this I learned:
when faced with forked paths
choose both
no book is ever finished
every mountain belongs to another
when we read each other across this
twilight softened range, we are,
become one,

beyond one.

what the scalphunter said

a fifth of tequila helps you with
finite
faster than
love or
fate.
Mezcal
is like happily
marching
into hell
with
scorpions
lighting
your way.

A Couple of James McMurtry Songs Later

I woke up in Organ Pipe National monument
on a chorus of meadowlarks
morning, hawk's cry,
coyote's plaintive yip carried on
the breeze across my tent, into
the dry Ajo hills-
                      a mug of spiked coffee and
a couple of James
McMurtry songs later, not
far from here, the Tohono O'Odom
angel of mercy leaves fresh water out
by the gallon and
fills emergency tanks everyday for
the border trekkers.

Some days the containers are slashed,
some days during drought, coyotes or
javalinas chew on the spigots, tongues
lathered for the last impoverished drop.

Wildfire smoke bleaches out the sun.
I think how McMurtry has the perfect Texas
voice for satire and pain, there's an angel in his
throat drunk on love and wine; I can
see the billows of dust kicked up by the
border patrol truck swallow

the Indian family
out there in the cacti
making the pilgrimage
to Padre Kino's grave.

No secret, dust devils of a
common anguish
erupt alongside mother beauty,
who drips scarlet
ocotillo blossoms all over these
dry disquieting
border desert mornings.

the roaring stillness across open ground

I'm kicking up the desert dust with my two dogs
on the kind of dry crisp morning
that draws the blue sky down around
it, everything that exists under it
the hummingbirds
spanish bayonet
the enflamed loose ends of summer, the

yellow snakeweed, the bahia
blossoms bobbing in the breeze
like rogue stars. The
emergence myths that rise from
the earth in ghost vendettas of
language.
The piney smell of the hike
resuscitates us
mothers us into knowing
these rituals come with the territory-
where we're amazed at the proximity
of faraway war,
its roaring stillness across open ground:

lone rufous hummer
destined for Mexico
last supper of the summer at
our plastic nectar blossom,

controlled burn-colored body hovering:
thinks I'm the chief flower of my species
crisscrosses my Hawaiian shirt like
a bandolier,
signifying a farewell of sorts,
the last of his tribe still this far north
from the Crossing of the Fathers to
the Rio Grande
a thousand heartbeats per minute

miles to go before real peace.

Cochise's Confession
-for J.K.

History re-invents itself dreaming
of procreating tiny histories that re-
invent themselves in mirrors of a vast pentagon;
thus,
    there
              is no waste. Yes we are anarchists, tilting
at fate,
but in the Thomas Merton sense. If
you can't have a revolution
in the
hospice of your quiet mind
where the fuck will it happen?
I turned Corso on to Merton
who said
meditation ain't shit
without a decent bourbon.
I scan all the vices of the desert's
dolorous miscellany.

On some mornings, I swear,
I'm crazier than Cervantes.

nirvana desperados

-in memoriam: Lew Welch

thirty six years ago you
left a turkey buzzard poem,
took your rifle,
disappeared into the Sierras, your
bones were stone mirrors no one
could find, the
crows buried your effigy.
You
    reaffirmed the art of clarity in poetry
re-ignited its beautiful crime for just
a minute;
since then, the inmates run the asylum,
an assortment of dirty
little wars,
the scent of lilac, woodsmoke.

In northern New Mexico
the stray light of yesterday's forked lightning
ignited the sun washed hills
like a paralyzing kiss while the sky
thundered over the house;
my wife knelt
down in an Aztec lamentation to
pray with the dogs.

Geronimo sent his loose confederacy of
Chiricahuas into the Sierra Madre camp two,
three at a time to surrender,
they blinked away the
twilight 's rare rain,
squatted near the flames
swapping stories,
fire gigglers, lamented these
end times and
re-ignited the beautiful clarity
of the rogue life /
                    full of grace.

Nana, Chato, Chihuahua
the others, warriors in the
extreme,
their shadow flames echo
across the summer universe.

the blues drink yr dreams away

                              -for Tony Scibella

surrogate mother of a morning
the dawn is a suttee,
a chaos pyre,
the clouds an armada of
fossil scorpions;
her beauty is *this* deep
as the desert drags a
dry razor
across her face;
the summer warmth bathes
her old bones in the spring pool.

                    In the remote
Dos Cabezas,
the feral dogs follow her to the
precipice where she can see the
Steller's jays preen like
hooded executioners.
This species of smoke signal is
extinct, speaks in border
language;
            the wind
carries interrogation ragas of American
neo-torture to
the bluecoats who sing to Jesus

as if he was *still* a carpenter but
war is alive and well,
living in Sonora,
in bad need of a shave.   The
autumn leaves
are dry, they scatter us like
ghost souls-

a straggled flock of musical bush tits
disguised as
tiny peace seraphim
cavort in this landscape
juniper to juniper.
The norte americano, lying on his
belly on the ballial,
binoculars pointed north
whispers to himself:

                      sometimes it's just as simple
as shooting fish in a barrel
as *holdin' up the end of the bar*
listening
to the wail
of man singing in the night

the blues drink yr dreams away.

Somewhere Between Arikara and Ft. Union
-a blue riff for Ed Dorn

It must've been a gibbous moon night
when European smallpox first explored the
Mandans before the warmth of the American
morning baked the fresh forest smell out of the air.

This morning, I watched a red tailed hawk
explore Canoncito floating circuitously,
burning daylight in the abstract,
a pound of flesh in her bloodless claws.

Down on the barranca earth
when the tv host asked the 100 year-old
man for the secret of his longevity,
he replied, *Don't die.*

Borrowed time in Chaco Canyon
-with a line by Ted Berrigan

For no particular reason,
borrowed time has given us
another day
upright on the earth,
in all of its exhausted duskiness
and anxious ancient first lights
of morning:
the serene immutability of
eternity, the sunlight piled
up in the doorway, here
in these greathouse ruins
of the canyon.

This must be where real peace abides,
where they keep the blood mysteries
in the deep kivas and the burning
yellow bulging chamisa
roadsides of September.
All forty-nine years of me trudged seven
miles to Penasco Blanco and back,
where an eight hundred year old shaman
tried to pray away the killer drought
at the nexus of river and desert
with a fresh macaw feather in his hair.

I thought of fire-breathing
Charles Bowden
author of *Blood Orchid* and

Blues For Cannibals
deconstructing
/reassembling
border consciousness,
who marched in the
summer heat across the Sand Tank
mountains to Gila Bend carrying a fist-
full of water, serene in the cold sweat of his ritual –
because it was there.

This is where real peace resides:
with these bellowing clouds that
melt like whispers on the dry horizon over
Chacra Mesa,
its pottery shards,
fossil sea shells,
parrot feathers,
copper bells and bird points,
the furnace hell of the far ruin in the hiking heat
eating peanut butter on wheat bread
upright against an Anasazi wall
every brick whispers:
all time is simultaneous.

I listened carefully, I could hear a
scorpion cast its shadow on the bare
slickrock and a flute-voiced woman
singing in the river:

*This is what we do. This is living,
taking its walk.*

jaguar sighting in northern Mexico

is like smoking the dust
of the past or
catching a glimpse of some
elusive rose of desolation
passing stealthily
from one dimension to another
up here
while the heat rattles
all of our skeletons
she's survived
her lost habitat is
scorned &
    scoured by the wind

ventures one
    breath at a time
into hostile territories of epic drought
with their howling cartel dogs of
encroaching nowhere
queen of the Sierra Madre
she's the only mountain lion
that roars!

Until Billie Holiday's voice opens up
its last remaining vein of dreams
until language becomes

total hallucination
until an overpopulated world
catches a few rays on
antarctic beaches of ash

el jaguar
        will be besotted with
outlaw singularity!

will be smoldering borderlands'
living proof spirit
blanched into translucence by
the night moon

leaves no tracks.

Territorial Sunday Best

territorial rattler in his
diamondback best
between me & the arroyo
morning loop trail ablaze
with first heat
he crosses another
                      ancient path to
citizenship
without reward

no ceremony
no coil
no rattle
shade hedonist
flicking tongue
knower of abstract
truths
everything else a formality.

In sweetwater, texas they wrangle
them out dead by the den full.

In a few steps I'm beyond
his range

on this *desierto*
we've satisfied basic notions
of community &
subsistence:
the casual permissions
of a summer's
day.

global warning

October is warmed by
siroccos
from the holy land &
I feel
dried out like an ancient
lake bed.
The leaves are projectile points
engorged with dried blood that
fill our Indian summer with
half-spirited dreams &
the elongated
heat propels the wind
illegal ivory trade
& guns across the
desert.   Issues disinterred
Rimbaud poems.
An orgy of assassins.

Comes from the
horse latitudes
a dreary, howling thing,
indivisible in the sky
without premise
or reason,
on the burning

wings of global warming,
on the backs of
calving ice shelves,
that fall into the ocean
endangered tusks
of a
merciless sky.

Winter Solstice

At my house,
Raul and I unload his pick-up
full of cedar logs and kindling, all green,
it'll dry for
the rest of the year,
for next September's first fire.
    Raul says cedar is hard, slow burning
wood, the perfect dead of winter
fuel. Each
log I pitch into the pile is like a confession
of a tiny sorrow or blessing,
for what I've got or forgotten what
I should have, for the bonds
of love that attach themselves
to my life,
stumbling elder in the dark,
how New Mexico must be the center
of the Hopi's universe.

For last night's full eclipse that blackened
the earth, and dawn's
slow exhalation of light
I toss a log,
and for this
morning, startling a red-tailed hawk trying to
get at the chipping sparrows hidden in

the firethorn: to them
the universe, a sanctuary,
the giving thing.
I toss a log.

   Or the Jesus, Mary and Joseph eyes
that followed me from crèche to
confessional as we stood, captive
second graders, guarded by pachydermatous
nuns, waiting in
that perfectly groomed devout and
snickering queue for the monsignor
to hear our first sins.
I toss a log.

   Today, the universe exists at about eye level:
a mound of green cedar, the December air, Raul and I in
a seasonal exchange of trucks, wood and weather,
that was
      getting colder as we stood there

perfect fuel for the dead of winter.

Sierra Oscura

And then, in this wearisome nowhere, all of a sudden,
the ineffable spot where the pure too-little
incomprehensively changes,—springs round
into that empty too-much?
Where the many-digited sum
solves into zero?
                        -Rilke

Those of us here
young, old
every color, strafed
veterans of some conflagration
or another
no protests out loud
only the private practice
                    of
                        open ground.

That first bomb day the morning star
descended as if into a far ocean
that hoards morning stars
until we *believed*
& then dispersed
them back into the war blackened
cosmos with the intensity
of a thousand suns. One
road enters ground zero the

straight & narrow path of the labyrinthine
invisible irradiated holy ground under
our fingernails
   blistering betrayer of dawns.

The undiluted desolation of those dark
uninhabited mountains,
the sierra oscura conceived in flames
the rattlesnake's ten thousand
years of stories to tell
the mesquite roots need wings
to reach deep water.
I look to the east
to ease their medicine in
I touch the cool
lava rock obelisk,
& feel my dimensions apportioned
into some
temporary whole.

They hung it a silent 100 feet above
the earth, dusky delinquent of the
feral wind, the bright white
bone dead dada moon held its
longest breath & watched us
  68 years later
mill about in the soullessness
of the blast radius.

Now, the morning heat fires up this sacred
now I am become death desert
forsaken by most gods,
but Keats,
who said the poetry
of earth is never dead —

under pale grey skies
without dimension,
the virga of
peace
        evaporates
before it reaches ground.

        —*Trinity Site, April 6, 2013*

The Day I Die

Christian, Jew, Muslim, shaman, Zorastrian, stone ground, mountain, river, each has a secret way of being with the mystery . . .
                —Rumi

will be the 2nd most important day
of my life
everyone else will be slouching
towards some end or beginning
there will be something
to look forward to
or nothing at all
Malcolm Lowry will still
be dead
but Popocatépetl's smoke
& ash can still be seen by
Monteczuma as
ghost language.
A few hummingbirds won't survive
the journey to backyard
nectar, most will,
most will continue to pray for
no more Verdun's or Gettysburg's
some won't
war will always be an option
peace a luxury
the post office will fall the way

of the pony express &
news of my death won't
spread far or wide but what most
people on earth don't know
a predator drone will tell them. I

will have survived most of my dogs.
Most of my power animals are
extinct except the mexican jaguar &
diamondback rattler
extinction being a long term solution
to a badly mishandled short term crisis.

A man in Santa Fe will wear his new
Hawaiian shirt for the first time & for
her first time, a teenager in Peoria
slips out of her lace panties. Somebody
will have demeaned an entire race with
a slur while somebody else once wrote:
something woven from the filaments of the past.

A few will have their executions stayed
most won't. There
will still be great beauty
great ugliness
& they will remain equal
      parts of the same unifying, staggeringly
wondrous whole

small men like rough beasts
will still crawl across the wasteland
to be reborn as sphinxes or
small kings & not one indignant
desert bird's wind shadow will cross
their stone eyes.

Some will be better at this than me
accosted by all manner of the body's
rude trespasses or life's
long game
shortened
each day
by a breath or two,
myriad churlish infirmities
glowering just
outside the window.

At its best
life is one long
sound check

the peril & wonder of rising
each day to the untroubled
air or some cold hell
of a wind
to save the whales
the desert tortoises
or visit grand cayman

while reading Creeley
his prayers
        his perfect eye
firmly
on life's memory & presence.

We will all go gently & not quite
into that good night
a poem will still leave its breath
on many windows,
will cut through the
soul's viscosity,
through the dust & ruins
to a place beyond my own border wire
to the mystery of dreams.

La Risa Café

we spread the domestic entirety
of our lives together on the table
amidst the newspapers and Sunday
breakfast of
        La Risa Café
Ribera, NM
next to the Pecos river
something about the red chili
stone floor
primitive chic architecture
of the patio
the warmth of summer
these
    last describable things
that made me
want to write this with
the invisible ink of memory
and rain freshened
river waters
of love.

        —*to Annie*

*

Japanese Volcano

late snow flutters down
each singular flake
a flower petal
a performance
adrift

any increase in stature or
population is one winter's
short ride up La Bajada hill,
where they fall as
whispers on the tongue or wild
& silent things
like Hiroshige's birds

still fluttering now
only more so
with the solemnity
of ash.

tracking the words

this evening
night hit the ground running,
there were star fields
    of questions
no echo answered,
just this solitude   this
exercise
in virtues of consciousness.
For you, Neruda
it was the white hot killers
of angry Spain
and the Chilean blood of
deserts,
for me, maybe
it is this old stone house
first made of air,
the Rio Grande running broad
and full, a jungle
of a bosque,
the low brow humor
of coyote;
in the whisper of a shooting
star parched from a million
mile crawl across
the universe.

Or does it come from
The rain that often struck your words
filling them with holes and birds?

Some nights I am at a loss for them,
when I should be soused with them or
at least tracking them through
the night, across the moon or
down desert rivers to their source.

after The Fall of America

dueling
buddhas
on the bookshelf,
a bad politics morning
drains the trees of their
hot colors. The wind carries
news of the cease fire, I sit on a rock

take solace in Ginsberg's
dispatches from all over
this indocile planet &
solitary autumn leaf
New England
trembles over
Kerouac's
grave.

Sacred Clown

trickster
Ezra Pound
in Rapallo,
his autumnal grey beard
softened
by the sea spray,
was jailed for
blowing mouth
in fascist Italy.

All is forgiven,
even his blind faith,
his trespasses,
his controlled burns;
holding court at St. Elisabeth's
    old & wild hearted,
when I look back on his
life I see the
mischievously joyless
eyes,
that say

What thou lovest well remains

& the day before his death
he walks down the
stairs unaided,
each step a foot of pride,
to the waiting
ambulance.

August in the Spanish Earth

These are the dog days of summer,
the heat has formed unholy
allegiances,
Lorca the pacifist was shot
on an August day at the foot
of the Sierra Nevada,
he prayed sweat into his
own grave, his
murder unmarked and late for his
funeral that never
showed up. We
leave memory to the
indigenous ghostliness of
the bones,
to these last days of deliberate warmth,
the field overgrown,
the orchard harvested,
the fallen peaches rot and sweeten
the air
and the last of the deliberate
angels give each other the first
of Last Rites,
but the words have risen and
wandered
away forever in time
from the Spanish earth.

Paris Elegy #1

Cendrars

The years behind are
receding, they won't be coming
back

*I think life has
hallucinated me*

Blaise Cendrars is here
in his tattered smoking jacket with
leather elbow patches,
hand-rolled hanging out of
the corner of his mouth,
smoke fills his book room
like morning mist
rising from the Seine. His right
arm was blown off in the
French foreign legion. He
wrote *Moravagine*. Pals with
Apollonaire. I excuse myself to
look at the ice-chipped river while
Blaise listens to Lotte Lenya sing
Mack the Knife
                on the phonograph.

Paris Elegy #2

Any place where I can
locate my ground
my center ring
the sound of me   will
surely outlast or
outclass me

the beat hotel
in the latin quarter
smelled like hashish &
Gregory Corso's
bathrobe.

Paris Elegy #3

dollhouse of mama war
—Gregory Corso

I stood with Gregory's ghost
on a bridge over the Seine
he was unshaven
shivering
in his bathrobe, lived
on the rue git le Coeur,
hit me up for ten francs,
we murmured scenes from our
childhoods into its
dark waters.

Later we ate coffee cake
he hit my first wife up for
ten francs,
it's as if we could hear
every heart's murmur
in the city,
doll's city
dope city
impressionist's palate
of sky

remembers us as children
remembers us at war.

Mexico Elegy

we talked surrealist-shaman
    poet Philip
Lamantia somewhere in Mexico
on this
moonspilled planet
searching for
peyote and mysticism,
his mind an aviary
of exotic musings,

was converted back to Catholicism
by a scorpion sting in
a last breath
campfire hallucination
where he wrote,

the mermaids have come to the desert.

Midwinter's day
—*after d.a. levy*

I.

We finish our chili verde,
frijoles, a twelve dollar bottle of
vino, you can hear the ping of our
glasses across the universe.
We've been here before,
just her & I,   another night
on the discomfited planet,
leave the one or two things better
left unsaid,
unsaid,
the wine is summer warm,
we relish its sincerity, we
progress gingerly from emotion
to emotion & in the ambling
circuitous nature of things,
come back to each other
on a deep starry black
                night, when the
fire in the old Scandia
sizzles & pops,   the sage
cross on it smokes so
slightly, its aroma tenders reflection,
an antidote to even the
subtlest of estrangements.

II.

Before the wine's gone
the underground horses & old
warriors shaking death rattles
will rise
       & take a wild last breath
ride with the devil across the
terrain of
absolute solstice darkness
called the poem,

the
humpbacked
universe will return to earth the
children taken too soon by guns,
Mexican wolves will laugh
at the moon,
no Mayan apocalypse now,
this *certain slant of light*
reveals mystery over form,
reveals poet
d.a. levy lived to be an old man,
his longest night collaged with peace
moonlight & words,
                his
hometown
Cleveland cancelled its NRA
membership & invited all of its
Indians
home for Christmas.

Angels Broken Down in Denver

I.

I once worked Larimer Street,
it sliced north and south through town
to the South Platte river,
serrated-edged winds
blew wild and grisly down from Wyoming,
blew newspaper shards and ghost
flesh down the alleys.

Sundays, the trees exploded with birdsong.
Instead of church I'd read Robin Blaser,
who wrote part of a poet's
spiritual discipline
is to be touched by the dark.

The angels laid them away:
freezing, debris field faces
occupied the street,
traded electric razors for wine,
free to be devoured by the wind,
boxcar woman sprawled by the
railroad tracks,
                I could see her head wound from a
block away, her hair a ghost crow frenzy of black feathers,
downwind from Wind River, out of the cold,
in and out of Indian time,
her blood flowed into the DNA of Larimer Street.

Front page from yesterday's newspaper
in some other language,
still blows against her body;
an election year, the headlines endorsed the apocalypse
        but misspelled grief.
Nothing would ever heal me if not for these unraveling
threads of our common spirit.

The railroad bars, and the red brick walls,
with faded graffiti scrawls of desolation,
moaned with neglect.
Neon signs over bereft sidewalks,
over the El Chapultepec: *Tonight! Thomas Tilton on drums,
D Minor on bass!*
had the temerity to flicker on and off and finally
Out, because Jesus didn't save that night,
because the souls were untouchable and
blew down the street that night,
because the night was stubbornly
American, because
the mariposa, lily of the barrio,
bloomed, sang out loud and then
died an angel's death,
because it's not hard to
give the city your blessing
because it's a mother,
    a jewel,
        a place of worship,
            a jazz trio,
                living proof Jesus loves
    dead places,
    a sentient being.

II.

After Creeley

Whenever I return the echoes breathe deep,
leave their own music behind on the way out.
I don't know how to say these things,
if I should, how
long I might stay here, thinking about you,
that day 28 years ago, you gave off so little heat,
your grey hair more wisps of smoke
than hair, in a room nobody should
belong to, even facing the pale
light of the window was a kind of scourge,
a few labored breaths away
from a summer
butterfly's
tranquility,
her music just above the ground.

I still feel
tender, semi-
articulate flickers
of your
presence . . .

I didn't know how far my vocabulary would
get me or how far
you'd drift away from us

when the summer sky didn't care
where the mariposa lily ended
and eternity began,
all the earth's butterfly's that survived
the chemicals and killing fields,
flickered with unforgettable fire.

Artaud in Mexico

He tells the dubious Tarahumara
Rimbaud never met a French poet he
didn't disdain.
Eats peyote by the handful
from a painted gourd,
has a vision of the nativity of Hieronymus Bosch,
dances the night away with
peyote sorcerers,
intuits the last words Sam Peckinpah
spoke to god,
reads A Season in Hell
by firelight
next to a graveyard
with its
lyrical colored metal crosses
and plastic
flowers;
chants, *one must be absolutely*
modern
as the incantatory clouds climb like
smoking gun blossoms high over
the Sierra Madre.

The Indians have mercy on this
tattered schizoid soul, install his
junkie ass upright on a drunken mule
for the long road home.

They recognize a kindred spirit
when they see one,
his garish, provocative nature not
at all at odds with
the fellaheen.

They dig his otherworldliness,
his seer's heart.

The Terminal Bar and Cafe

I drank there a few times while I worked the docks, driving a truck. Vintage, tragic, smokier than the history given off by graves place: the down-and-outers, the Us, The Other, the End. One lectured me how every bar and cafe should sell single cigarettes at the counter. He used to sing *Too-ra-loo-ra-loo-ral* lovingly on the barrio sidewalk and wave at me as I drove past. He was always shaking from the booze or shivering from the cold. Says one day the train just dropped him off on old Blake Street. He had the Blake Street shakes and the boxcar blues. Says an old girlfriend tried to slit his throat in his sleep. He fell out of love with her. He used to be a brakeman on the railroad until he broke his back one cold midnight in the switching yard. An owl kept him company until he was found the next morning. Says he could see the bird's breath in the moonlight and it kept him alive. That day, he swore off whisky swore to the Irish saints, I'll stay dry. One night, in a flophouse

hotel, a broken man breathed the tragedy of his life all over him. They each had lost a son to Vietnam. He hasn't been sober since. He answered to no higher power but he listened to the spiders from Mars, they told him the saints had averted their eyes.

vespers

I scour these territories before they become lamentable with wild fires, some selective, some hysterical as if attempting to exorcise their demons with promiscuity. I rode my stingray with the banana seat on the edge of the desert in my mind for years before the drought drove me indoors. Washington is lousy with charlatan lowlifes but this garden defies climate change and barters with the gods for permission to extoll the virtues of its cutthroat beauty. I was raised a catholic because our family had an ecumenical view of pain and suffering. The young lady who sells newspapers on the street corner complains about the weather and tells me her last name in her native Ethiopian means *Mother of Rains*. My mother is long gone and we missed vespers for the thousandth time. My behavior in God's eyes, though lamentable is, I'm sure, on the edge of redemption. Prayer is being able to not only share breakfast with a black-chinned hummer, first of the dry spring, but a mystery, and a window. Upon reflection, a moment's notice.

Creeley

Reading his lines, a measure
of his then immaculate now, each
one, make no mistake, a
vow, a bright continuance. A
long life of trees, for instance,
and their companionships. Whether
Helsinki or Placitas, he was always
an oracle of place. Summer or
winter, it all rooted him deep in
humanity. Taking ten minutes to
write it, master of his craft, thirty
seconds for me to read it: *what
is truth firm (as a tree)*,
an eternity, old friend, to
dream it in.

Ventriloquist Rock (Colorado)

There are two filament delicate fawns in the camouflage
    game trail overgrowth silence.
I climb to the top of a rock I haven't touched in thirty five
    years. A moment as implicit in time
as memory would allow. I could've been on Easter Island with
    the moai or in a house of worship, stoned into sentience
and surrounded by million year old water. A fetish the size of
    Empire. A ground of being.
The rock doesn't recognize discord or asylum, just wildflowers
    and fires, but only in the abstract.
Its existence is the resistance, no American ghosts can be seen
    passing through it. The best words
bounce off its rough face and flail on the ground like abandoned
    meth children of the bloodshot earth.
This is where I made myself up before I lived it all down, where
    I was impressed with my mercurial unworldliness.
I sit and listen to all the years I've lived in between, the white
    noise from the filament delicate creek below
or voices from a bereaved land. Thirty-five years later I wept
    reading *The Deer Lay Down Their Bones*. Maybe
someday it'll be some septuagenarian dictator's death mask:
    the rigor suits him.
The others, never to be exhumed, lie busy waiting.

Award- winning poet/playwright/essayist John Macker lives in Santa Fe, NM. His latest publications are *Gorge Songs* (DCArt Press, 2017) with Denver woodblock artist Leon Loughridge and *Blood in the Mix* (with El Paso poet Lawrence Welsh) Lummox Press, 2015. In 2014 *Disassembled Badlands* was published (the 3rd book in the *Disassembled Badlands* trilogy) and available at fine local bookshops. Other books include *Woman of the Disturbed Earth, Underground Sky, Adventures in the*

Gun Trade, Las Montañas de Santa Fe and *The Royal Road: Impressions of El Camino Real* (both in limited edition and with woodblock art by Leon Loughridge). In 2006, he edited the *Desert Shovel Review.*

John was the recipient of *Mad Blood Magazine's* 2006 first annual literary arts award for the long poem, *Wyoming Arcane.* He's also the recipient of the 2001 Colorado Arts *Tombstone* Award for poetry, presented in Denver. He has been awarded a Colorado Council on the Arts grant for his arts periodical, *HARP* and has been nominated for 2 Pushcart Small Press Prizes. His recent essays on poets and poetry can be found in New Mexico's *Malpais Review* (where he is contributing editor) and *Cultural Weekly,* and his essay on the late pop artist John Chamberlain, *Without Fear or Crowbars* was published in the 2016 Chamberlain exhibit catalogue, *Wickets*. He recently presented a paper on the late novelist Frank Waters at the Harwood Museum in Taos, sponsored by SOMOS.

Has worked as a journalist and given readings, lectured and taught workshops at colleges and festivals throughout the West, including El Paso Community College, Sparrows Poetry Festival, *Venus in the Badlands,* Santa Fe, NM, Colorado Mountain College, Colorado Mesa University, Edward Abbey Conference, Moab, Utah; Aspen Institute, Aspen, CO, Karen Chamberlain Poetry Festival, the Harwood Museum, Taos, NM, the Duende Poetry Series and Ziggie's Poetry Festival in Denver. In 2009, his books were featured in *A Mile High and Underground*, an exhibit of Denver literary history, Auraria Campus, sponsored by the Colorado Historical Society.

www.ingramcontent.com/pod-product-compliance
Lightning Source LLC
Chambersburg PA
CBHW020124130526
44591CB00032B/516